Write and REwrite

A writer's guide to start writing
A writer's wish to see others write more

Garima Chauhan

Copyright © Garima Chauhan 2025
All Rights Reserved.

ISBN 979-8-89588-395-2

"Writing is a way of talking without being interrupted."

– Jules Renard

Contents

Introduction

Half of your beauty lies in your words.

"Verba volant, scripta manent" is a Latin proverb, which translates into "(spoken) words fly away, written ones remain". So, if there is anything that is permanent, it is written communication because oral words will disappear once uttered. The permanency of words is often contrasted with the impermanence of everything else. So, if you want God to bless you, ask him to bless you with the power of words.

"The pen is mightier than the sword", first written by Edward Bulwer Lytton, also stresses the importance of mind over might.

We have been on this Earth for far too long to have seen everything. Moreover, the world has seen brutal wars which destroyed the buildings. We have seen changes, which make it difficult to understand what was there before. But what has survived is what was written. Religions which were written survived. Literature which was written survived. Tribes which did not have a written tradition perished.

So it turns out that words may well last longer than stone and have more impact than mighty empires.

PART 1

GOOD WRITING MOVES YOU

I was listening to one of my favourite songs, "Kun Faya Kun" from the movie *Rockstar* and decided to check out the comment section for fun. It was full of love towards the song. Some of the comments were: what beautiful lyrics; I always come back to this song whenever I feel low; the lyrics give me peace as if I have just prayed; the lyrics motivate me to surrender and have faith in God. And I just realised how lucky the lyricist and the singer are to receive this; to know that someone listens to the song every day as a form of their prayer, their words have given people hope, faith, and sometimes stopped them from taking their lives. How beautiful.

And that's when I realised words move people in a way that nothing else can. They make people feel what's written on the paper. A single well-written line can evoke tears, laughter, or deep reflection. And the ones who can do it are called the real artists or, in today's lingo, the real deal.

Nowadays, when a movie hits big, the director says the writing was the real hero, and when the performance is deeply moving, it's like, "Hey, I acted well because it was all written on the paper."

The greatest power a writer has is that they can make a person feel heard. So many people resonate with the hero when he struggles to pay the rent, fights with his wife, or cries at his daughter's wedding.

In *The Pursuit of Happyness,* when Will Smith's character finally lands a job, it made thousands of grown-up men cry as they recalled their struggle of supporting their families. In *Dead Poets Society,* when the professor inspires his students to pursue literature, took me back to the moment I decided to choose literature over the sciences. For example, when someone argues that divorce is taken by people who run away from responsibilities, they bring up *Marriage Story* to show how painful the process really is. When discussing how hubris can lead to downfall, they might mention *Titanic* or *Frankenstein*. Words are so powerful that they become the lens through which you see the world. Hence, people often use art to defend themselves.

When you are in a self-growth phase, you consume good movies (self-help, spiritual, philosophical) and books to learn. You look for answers in them, and many times, you are lucky enough to find them too.

We are creatures who feel everything. A writer is gifted because they can feel, observe from a third-person point of view, express it in words, knowing very well that it would evoke the same feeling in the person reading it as they felt when writing it. This transference of feelings through words is the wizardry of an artist.

The magic of a writer lies in shifting our perspectives. Sometimes it is not even about creating new thinking; it's just the ability to write something which everyone thought, and oftentimes about expressing truths we think but are afraid to say out loud. For example: The seeds of the Protestant Reformation were sown in 1517 when Martin Luther publicly posted his 95 theses on the door of the Castle Church in Wittenberg. It was a single piece of paper that shook the foundations of Christianity and led to the reformation of the Church. He brought individualism to the centre of the religion, where earlier pope and practices of Catholicism were. If he stood against the church, what did he stand on? Holy Scripture, written words, *Bible*. He religiously read *The Psalms* (sacred poems/songs) and completed it every three weeks. He believed the words in it would save mankind and not the preachings of Christianity. Naturally (and unfortunately) he was excommunicated from the Church in 1521.

Another important landmark moment of English history is Romanticism, the period which glorified individuality and emotion over tradition and rationality. And it all started with one book: *Lyrical Ballads* published by William Wordsworth and Samuel Taylor Coleridge. Wordsworth's "Preface" to the second edition of *Lyrical Ballads* became a manifesto for the movement. Artists came to be seen as 'cultural leaders' and as P.B. Shelley famously said, "Poets are the unacknowledged legislators of the world."

We're all moulded by our upbringing, parents, friends, school, peer group, which shapes our thought process and trains us to see the world in a certain way. But, when an artist sees through the hypocrisy of structures and sees things for what they really are, not just what he's been trained to see, he becomes a true writer. Free from all and any notions of prejudice and personal gain, he stops classifying things into black and white and presents the truth as it is, raw and unfiltered.

Being an introvert, writing has given me a way to feel heard and a safe space to express. In my childhood, I had an overwhelming fear of judgement for saying things that won't go well with the audience. But now writing has given me the confidence to talk to people without meeting them.

Writing has also given me so much more perspective and clarity on the smallest of things around me.

Each person, with their memories, perceptions, and beliefs, is a universe in themselves, and writers are the only people who, through their words, can shake the foundations of someone's beliefs.

Art? It shakes things up – your thinking, emotions, state of mind, and can even bring a revolution. But you know what's really tough? Convincing someone they were wrong. It's like squaring a circle. Believe it or not.

The greatest power of an artist, according to me, is that an artist not only can create something already existing but can also create something never seen or heard before without even logically justifying or explaining themselves. Next thing you know, everyone's talking about it, debating about it, and suddenly, you've got a whole 'cult following' on your hands. Just look at what happened with *Harry Potter*, *Lord of the Rings*, and *Game of Thrones*. People live in a parallel world of *Harry Potter*, sorting themselves into Hogwarts houses, creating fan theories, throwing costume theme parties, and waiting at King's Cross Station on 1 September to hear a fictional announcement for the start of a fictional term at a fictional school 'Hogwarts'.

If we go back in time, we have Shakespeare, who has given us themes like 'star-crossed lovers in Romeo and Juliet', 'jealousy in Othello' and 'power and madness in King Lear'. Shakespeare seems to have a doctorate in psychology without even having been to a university or having a degree. Jane Austen has done a favour to all young girls around the world by giving them idealistic fictional men whom they romanticise and idealise over. All her books are adapted into serials, movies, and spin-offs, to the extent of being overdone. Modern-day concepts like 'the big brother is watching' (George Orwell, *1984*); 'newspeak' (George Orwell, *1984*); 'Catch-22' (Joseph Heller, *Catch-22*, 1961); 'Kafkaesque' (Franz Kafka, *The Trial*, 1925); 'Time Machine' (H.G. Wells, *The Time Machine*, 1895); 'Frankenstein' (Mary Shelley, *Frankenstein*, 1818); and 'finding our ikigai' (It helps us understand the world we are living in). Do you know what's common in all of these?

They have been battle cries, part of pop culture and then part of our life. They have become a part of our dictionary, vocabulary, and language to understand and explain the world.

PART 2

GOOD WRITING EMPOWERS YOU

Chapter 1
It First Challenges You

The two things a person has to master are speaking and writing well. Both of these things make one more articulate. But is it easy? No. It is difficult. It is going to be challenging because if it were not, the world would be a more articulate place, but unfortunately, it is not. It is full of people who write bad emails, confusing reports, and messages that cause misunderstanding, and birthday wishes that do not sound heartfelt. And when you find someone who can read and speak well, you are deeply impressed and automatically assume them to be wise and well-educated, probably from a prestigious university or academic background or a subject matter expert in that field.

W. H. Auden said, "What the poet says has never been said before, but once he has said it, his readers recognise its validity for themselves." It is true because we all feel the same thing. What we lack is the skill to convert it into words. And that skill is acquired solely through writing and writing more. That comes with patience. Once we do, we realise that everyone was sailing in the same boat.

It is challenging, but it will help you find your voice that would be authentically yours. You might not be a famous writer or a professional, but no one else can think or write like you. It is amazing to think of because no one else can say what I have to say in the way I say it.

When you try to write and your vocabulary is limited, you struggle to find the right words to fit in. Then you google, ask a friend, or refer to a dictionary, and that's how you expand your vocabulary. You need that word as the last piece of the jigsaw puzzle. Your thoughts won't be complete without it. Words are like bricks in a house. The more bricks you have, the bigger your house is. Similarly, the more words you know, the more you understand yourself. Every feeling is different, and there are words for every feeling. The more words you know, the more you know yourself.

Isaac Asimov used to say that writing was thinking with your fingers. I couldn't agree more. Written words are organised thoughts. And once you have your thoughts organised, you can study them better and use them better. As writing is an introspective practice, an artist writes not for an audience but for himself. He wants to listen to himself in his own voice to understand himself better.

However, writing is challenging. Good writing challenges you because it forces you to get into the deepest recesses of your heart and dig out emotions, some very uncomfortable ones like jealousy, insecurity, and disappointment. And the feeling of laying yourself bare is not pleasant.

You always have an idea, ideology, or perspective that you stand by. And you want to defend it. When you argue about it verbally, it's not always very logical. Your emotions overpower it, you are scared of the person you are talking to because you want to be politically correct, and simply you don't get enough time to form an argument thought of by all sides when you are speaking. Once you write something, you have transferred your defence onto the paper. You can pat yourself on your back for creating a well-defined argument. That's your armour and shield. You have thought it through, from all the possible angles, made counter defences and now can stand by what you have written.

Be ready to back it up.

Once you do, and win that argument, everyone around you wins because they too believe it as their argument and defence on that particular topic.

Mirza Ghalib is a name known in every household. He was a gifted letter writer. He revolutionised both Urdu poetry and prose by making it enter every house. He wrote in easy and popular Urdu. Instead of making Urdu ornamental, he made it simple. He made his letters "talk" by using words and sentences as if he were conversing with the reader. According to Ghalib:

"From a thousand miles, talk with the tongue of the pen,

and enjoy the joy of meeting even when you are separated."

When I say writing is a kind of "self-help", I am the self. I'm just trying to help myself.

It also takes care of your spiritual health, as when you write, you write from and for your inner voice.

When you live your life, you are living only one life. But when you are reading, you are reading multiple lives.

Clear writing is a sign of clear thinking. Does this mean that you have to attend literature and grammar classes to be more effective when carrying out your tasks? No, you already have all the necessary knowledge. You need to incorporate writing. And you only learn how to write by writing more and often.

As a human, you are always listening to new information. But when you try to write down the information in your own words, you understand the concept better, and it stays with you for longer.

If you start writing about yourself every day, after a period of time you would understand who you are and you would not need others to do it for you. You would not need others to identify your patterns, weaknesses, and strengths, as you can see it for yourself on the paper. This will help you become self-aware, and you will eliminate stress; it's like a word vomit. When you carry too many things in your mind, it gets all entangled like a web. And you can't unjumble it in your mind. You need to take it out on a piece of paper and solve it like a puzzle.

I have had moments of utter confusion and senselessness in my life. But if not for writing, I would mess up even more. There are different ways to cope with an external problem. You will overcome difficult moments faster when you write about it versus if you don't write about it. You will be peaceful. This outcome is a direct benefit of the preceding two points.

Life is like standing under a scorching sun. And writing is a brief respite from the heat, the times when you find solace in the shade. In this fast-paced life, it is a challenge to slow down. But it becomes your moment of calm in the chaos.

You may have heard the saying "write about what makes you angry," and when you sit to write, you would not be able to write one logical, meaningful line. All you will see is gibberish on the paper. What most people consider thoughts are actually anger wrapped in cuss words.

When you try to turn your thoughts into words, you often find that those words do not fully capture your thoughts. Then, you have to keep writing, keep digging for the truth, until you've gotten past all of your emotional baggage and cognitive biases.

So, writing is the ultimate tool for self-discovery, which is the ultimate means to an authentic life. You can grow by researching, talking, and listening to smart people, but it will only add to your knowledge base. When we start writing, we move towards certainty, and the moment we begin to seek clarity, we begin to lose our certainties. As Socrates widely observed, 'The unexamined life is not worth living,' we need to examine our lives methodically, and writing is the best tool for that.

Chapter 2
Then It Empowers You

Remember how you have stored love letters and birthday cards from grade 5? When you hold that paper and read the words written in their handwriting, it transports you back to that feeling. Writing can store nostalgia. A paragraph can ignite memories in your heart and take you on a trip down memory lane. A lane whose gate you had locked with no will to enter, but that writing broke the lock and flooded you with nostalgia.

It empowers us in more ways than one:

1. **You're more likely to achieve written goals**

    Writing down your goals works like an alarm clock. It wakes up your brain and reminds you until you finish it. And you can't snooze that alarm or stop it. According to research from the Dominican University in California, "You are 42 percent more likely to achieve your goals if you write them down." These odds are worth taking. And I have witnessed it myself.

2. **Thinking for yourself**

    The best part about writing is that it empowers you. It pays you back. You can start thinking about yourself. Good writing makes you feel seen, heard, and understood. It's like having a one-on-one conversation with yourself.

3. **Writing doesn't have to be commercial**

Good writing is not judged by how much money it has made but how many people were moved by it that they could not help but share it. That's why YouTube/Instagram believes more in shares than likes on your posts. People's opinion on your writing doesn't matter. All that matters is if you have made someone feel validated by what they read. Instead of just giving them some information, you have touched people's innermost turmoil, dark emotions, fears, and insecurities.

4. **It helps to make better decisions**

This can be done by straightening out your thinking. And what's the easiest and quickest way to do it? By penning down your thoughts, juggling with them, wrestling with them, throwing away the pawns (read ideas), and keeping the strong soldiers who will defend you and fight for you against the other intruder thoughts.

5. **Bonding activity**

When you write, your writing touches people. Whoever reads it feels like sharing it with others to tell them how they feel because you have used the exact words to describe what they feel. It's a rare moment. It feels like you have transferred a part of yourself to others, and they have become an extension of yourself. You have developed a personal bond with them, an exclusive group of mutual feelings and perspectives.

It has become a trend to follow someone's writing. You create your own community of people who believe in what you believe and live by your words.

This creates a beautiful sense of community.

6.   Writing as a tool for healing

Not only can the artist heal himself or herself through art, but they can also heal others and offer them new ideas and new perspectives.

Art has been valued for a long time not only for its cultural value, but also for its therapeutic potential. It serves as a powerful tool for healing, both for the artist and for those who experience their work. A single piece of art can help you connect with a whole host of emotions.

It reflects the thought of the artist. So you can get closer to his/her thoughts as you comprehend the message. Art can thus be a great messenger of ideas.

Inspiration - This is what I love the most about art. It can inspire and motivate you to such an extent that the fire within you gets rekindled.

Your interest in life can be boosted to a great extent by a single masterpiece that has been able to influence you. Art we consume reflects the time we live in.

When you write better emails, memos, reports, presentations, and publications, your ability increases manifold. If there is an engineer who knows how to write well, he is a better employee and has more chances of rising up than the other ten in your office.

It helps in developing eloquent speeches, reports and presentations because everything you have said has already been thought about earlier and written down in some form or another.

7. **Your thoughts are more organised**

You can see the patterns in your thinking; once you have written it down, you can see which thought to keep and which one to discard and which one is creating a problem in your thinking and is affecting your outcome. You can also then add more thoughts in a particular order to streamline your thinking for a desired goal.

8. **It Gets Your To-Dos Out of Your Head**

David Allen, author of *Getting Things Done*, is famous for saying that your head is a terrible office. It's cluttered with incomplete tasks, disorganised, causing mental fatigue and decision paralysis. We actually can't store more than four action items in our heads at any point. So, free your brain by writing down all important things and referring to it instead of keeping it in your mind and relying on your memory to save you in the most crucial moment.

Sometimes you want to explain something to the other person, but you are yourself confused and lack words to do that. In that case, writing saves your life. You can write and edit and then give that piece of paper to somebody else to help them understand it easily. What is written goes a long way in understanding something.

9. **Writing clarifies your ideas in your head**

When I was younger, I had friends who had pen friends, and I always used to wonder how they could possibly develop a friendship with somebody whom they had never met. But I guess now I realise that communication is the only thing that sustains a friendship. Exchanging letters is one of the purest way of communicating with somebody.

10. **Writing is an important work skill**

No work can happen without communication. You are constantly communicating with your colleagues, boss, managers, trainers, and staff, and you do not want your poor communication skills to dilute your message or sabotage your work, which will directly undermine your authority and damage your reputation.

11. **Writing is a powerful tool for manifestation**

Now that we have included that manifestation works in real life, there are various ways of doing it, but it has been established that writing down something increases your manifestation power and makes it easy for you to create your life. When you speak things, you are saying a lot of things and the mind is treating it just like a chat. However, when you write down something, your mind sees what is important, registers it, and starts taking action based on that. So, it is always easier to manifest something that you have written than what you have said.

A lot of times when we are planning something, we become overambitious and create castles in the air. It's only when we write down the plans that we can actually see what is actionable, achievable, and realistic and what is not. It makes the journey easier after working on the idea.

Writing strengthens your creative muscles, which help you in the other areas of your life. When you tell your brain to write something and then rewrite and edit it, it helps your brain to become sharp, and that helps you to solve some other problems at home or work. Creativity is all interlinked, just like chess provides you with new perspectives towards different problems, writing increases your problem-solving skills and ability to see the structures behind it.

12. Understanding how to write can help you read between the lines

When you really understand how to write, you'll find yourself capable of reading between the lines. That helps to study people and their real motives.

Giving reviews has become a job. People make their purchases based on Amazon reviews, product reviews, customer feedback, and food reviews. People buy clothes with the maximum reviews. They form an opinion based on what somebody wrote on Facebook or Quora. People have become dependent on customer reviews and feedback because they rely on this source for every major decision. What's written on social media serves as the truth.

13. Writing Improves Social Skills

I know people who have saved their relationships by writing the best birthday cards, anniversary wishes, and farewell messages. It showed emotional intelligence in saving and sustaining the relationships. It made them come across as people-friendly persons with good social skills and often helped them overlook their mistakes.

Writing every day is one of the good habits that you can implement in your life like exercising every day, meditating every day, to keep yourself healthy. It is like eating healthy food every day, talking to your loved ones, listening to good music and content, or striking a balance between your personal and professional life.

14. Creative writing engages both sides of the brain

The right side of the brain is the more creative side, while the left side is the more analytical and logical side. You need both sides to do anything, but especially creative writing. The right brain handles all the visions of what you want on the page, and the left side helps you put it down in a way that makes sense.

15. It helps you think through problems

Whenever I'm feeling stuck or contemplating a problem, it helps to write it down and work through possible solutions on the page. This is especially helpful when writing longhand.

16. Written words influence society

Journalists, bloggers, speechwriters... How we think as a society is largely thanks to what people write. This is how propaganda works, through newspapers, speeches, articles, and letters. We form an opinion towards political parties based on what people tweet, we judge famous personalities' characters based on the interviews they give, we form an opinion on what's happening in the USA or Israel based on the editorial report in the newspaper.

17.   There is no history without writing

"History is written by the victors," is a popular saying. But if we didn't write it down, we wouldn't have it at all. I just wish more people would study history because if we don't, we're doomed to repeat it.

Another important thing we have because of this is our religious scriptures. The Gospel of Jesus wouldn't travel as far and as wide as it has today if the Biblical authors hadn't written it, nor would the Quran, Gita, or Torah.

18.   Everyone has a book inside them

I've had books inside me all my life. I think everyone has a book inside, whether they realise it or not. It's not necessarily a book of fiction. It could be a book of their experiences. Why do you think autobiographies are popular? People want to share their stories. And everyone has a story to tell. Writing is the only way to get that story into the hands of people who care.

19.   Writing gets the gunk out

Just like flossing removes gunk from between your teeth, writing removes gunk from between your brain cells. So if something is waking you up in the middle of the night, try writing it down.

By writing a personal diary or journal, you can release pent-up emotions like sadness, anger, or bitterness. You can write happy things down too – I try to write down one thing that I'm grateful for each day, for example.

20. **Writing builds authority**

Writing a blog about cycling made people think I was an expert. So, when you write about something, people assume that you know more about it than others, and that's an advantage you would not want to miss having.

Writing is also about authority. Written orders serve as proof; oral orders don't. Whatever you have given in writing can serve as proof or testimony. That's why all government and court orders are always written.

We have all heard folklores and have been told that they are hearsay. Stories which have been modified, changed, and edited to suit the narrator's perspective. And so is gossip; a bunch of oral unverified news.

21. **Writing makes ideas better: By writing down an idea so that someone else can understand it, it becomes clearer to yourself**

If you can't explain it to a six-year-old, you don't understand it yourself." - Albert Einstein

The act of writing forces you to get to the core of an idea. If your thinking is muddy, your writing will be too. But if you've found a way to write it down clearly, you can be sure that you're onto something good.

22.   **It helps in reviewing your thought process**

It is written and is therefore more permanent. You can keep coming back to a previous piece of writing, and you may gain more benefit from reviewing it as a result.

But... do remember that you do not have to submit your first draft. The writing process may take many forms (visually and textually) and looking back at your previous experiences of writing can help you learn more about your writing style.

Writing offers you time and space to redraft and refocus your message. In this way, perhaps, it is easier than spoken communication. When speaking, you have to think of words and immediately release them to the audience, and once spoken, there is no opportunity to 'edit' them before they are heard.

The process of writing is something that you can constantly learn from. This process will help you gain feedback and reflection on your writing that can help you develop as a writer. However, an important benefit of writing is also that as a form of assessment, a piece of writing can be used to measure our progress by reflecting on it again and again.

23.   **Writing creates room for debates**

Writing sometimes has more impact than other communication channels. Through writing, you can select language to influence the thoughts and actions of your readers in particular ways, guiding them through your evidence and argument to convince them of your analysis and conclusions.

Artwork is often created by an individual to express their emotions or ideas. However, the aim is not to convert the viewer but to simply encourage the exploration of a theme, to provoke a thought. Artists are creating an experience, hence why artwork is considered subjective.

Art is for anyone and everyone — because art owns everyone and not the other way around.

24.   Writing is an art of persuasion

Make art and make what you like. The greatest power of an artist is to influence a mass audience. The greatest power of a writer is their ability to communicate ideas, emotions, and experiences through their work. The Catholic Church has survived for centuries not by passing on a celibacy gene, but by passing on the stories of the New Testament and of Catholic canon law. It takes blood and sweat to write. I know. But it's worth every drop of that.

Chapter 3
Banishing The Excuses

What's with all those pesky excuses we make for not writing? Let's break them down.

Excuse 1: I am not a writer

If you mean a person who earns a living, then maybe you are not. A lot of us are not. But someone who has the ability? Then yes, you are a writer. And that's enough to write well.

Here's the writing paradox: You won't find out what you have to write about until you start.

We have sufficiently covered the points in the preceding chapters. You do not have to necessarily have something to say in order to write; you just need to wish to write in order to write.

Technology has made it easier to read. Consequently, it has also made it easier to write because you have an audience who is reading more. If we are reading more, of course, someone is writing more. And the audience is vast; it cuts across class, caste, race, gender, ethnicity, and nationality. Even if you share your smallest details—like your opinion on the pizza you ate—people would read even that. And written words are heard more. Try tweeting about your train delay or file an RTI; it's bound to have a prompt response.

Excuse 2: I do not have time

No one has time to write if they are not from the professional field of writing. It is quite obvious that you would not have dedicated time to write. However, it would get easier if you can shift your mindset towards using writing as one of the mediums of communication.

We have got used to using WhatsApp, talking to people, engaging in small talk, reading news on our phones, using social media, and reading. Technology has two modes of communication: listening and reading. Cheap recharges have made it possible for us to stay connected with loved ones and colleagues all the time. You are always listening to them and talking to them. Video calls have added one more layer of personal interaction. We can talk for hours while looking at each other. Technology has also made reading accessible and easy. For example, instead of newspapers, we are always reading on a phone through apps like Twitter, news channels, and social media statuses. Kindle has decreased the physical carrying of books. This has exponentially increased our reading and listening time. However, we have not yet inculcated writing into our modes of communication, and we are paying a price for it. We are getting more confused, our brains are freezing, and we are developing anxiety; it's difficult for us to make decisions. And it is all because we are bombarded with information from all sides but we have not yet developed how to filter it and selectively process what is beneficial for us and what is not. Writing is a fail-proof method to filter the junk, streamline our thinking process, and develop clarity of thoughts. If you cannot dedicate a regular slot for your writing, your phone has already given you multiple ways that you can use throughout the day to get into the habit of writing.

If later you realise that you have a flair for writing, you can start your own blog to write about the most random things which interest you like car washing or your favourite cartoon character or on spirituality or your cooking recipes or create a social media profile to write movie reviews, food reviews, restaurant reviews or use mediums like Twitter and Quora to write for an audience. You can also send newsletters to people. These are free-of-cost ways to write, develop an audience and see if you could make a professional career out of it.

Remember that writing is like a muscle that must be exercised to develop it. But you don't have to write every day. Even a weekly or twice-weekly writing slot will help. (I send an email newsletter every Sunday—or at least, I try to—because it forces me to write something useful once a week).

Jawaharlal Nehru wrote the book *The Discovery of India* during his imprisonment at Ahmednagar fort for participating in the Quit India Movement. Mahatma Gandhi wrote *The Story of My Experiments with Truth* during his imprisonment in Yerawada Central Jail in Pune, Maharashtra. Similarly, Winston Churchill also took pains to write. He had an impeccable writing schedule where he wrote every day for four hours, and then extensively edited and re-edited it. No wonder, he led the country to victory in WW2 and kept the hopes up through his memorable speeches like "fight on the beaches" and "blood, toil, tears, and sweat".

The writing format has also changed now. People are using fewer words to communicate. Abbreviations and acronyms are used (IKR - I know right, TBH - To be Honest), shortened phrases (TL;DR - Too long, didn't read, BRB - be right back), single-word reactions (Love!, Wow!), hashtags (#SelfcareSunday), text speak (u instead of you) and, in fact, emojis are used to communicate emotions. Social media has introduced features like reacting which has made it even simpler to leave our opinion. It's all because of the evolution of writing style which has taken over the internet. As people now have a reduced attention span and an increased need for quick bite-sized information to release dopamine, they have adapted writing to fulfil these conditions.

Excuse 3: My mind goes blank when I start writing

That's normal to happen when you start writing. You have so much going on in your mind that your mind gets overwhelmed. It doesn't know in which direction to write. Once you train your mind to write as you think, with practice, it becomes better. It will only get blank for a few minutes, and after that, it would automatically start giving you ideas, and you would get a running mind.

Excuse 4: Fear of judgement

If you are writing for yourself, no one else can read it. If you are writing for the public, focus on saying what you have to say and not how the audience receives it. If you have managed to write well, it's bound to get connected with your audience. If not, take it as genuine feedback and work on it, for it might be that your writing had gaps at that time. The rest are trolls, who are nameless and shameless people who don't care about feedback but only want to disrespect people. You don't have to focus on those.

People also write diaries with the intention of never publishing them. They hide them from their family, lock them, and keep them away in a secret place. They do it out of fear of judgement. And that's also okay. Not every writing has to be commercialised. People do it for themselves, and it serves their purpose.

Excuse 5: I am too tired to write

It's scientifically proven that writing relaxes your mind, relieves you of anxiety, straightens your thinking, and gives you clarity, which in turn calms you down and makes you confident. Art has started to be used in therapy to treat people suffering from various mental disorders.

Once you have clarity in your thoughts, nobody can manipulate you into their thinking.

PART 3

How To Make Your Writing Better

Can you judge a person just by the way they write, even if you have not met them or conversed with them? If I write an email to you or text over WhatsApp, you would make a fairly good estimate of my personality and judge me even before we meet. That's why people say that he or she was not like what I thought. Hence, writing makes your first impression even before you have met them first. With social media, we are writing more than ever and reading more than ever. We are continuously judging people based on their status, caption, birthday wishes, reels, posts or opinion on X. We think we know the entire person's personality, political affiliation, sexual orientation, religious views, environmental views just by assessing their content on social media, and without even having met once. Sharing one tweet can lead to massive trolling, which becomes a permanent record of their beliefs. It results in cancel culture, bans and career ruin. That's the power of 280 characters, for you.

To write better, read more. Read what everyone else has read, and then don't read what everyone else is reading. Talk to everyone, see the world from their perspective. Ask interesting people you meet to recommend books. Raid your parents' collection. Pick something at random from the bibliography of your favourite author. Reading is like a superpower. And when you can relate books to each other (combining what you learn from *Pride and Prejudice* with the latest book *It Ends with Us*, for example), then you will develop new patterns.

Any success I've had in life, I owe to reading a few books a week.

Plus, every book you read makes you write better. Learning to communicate is one of the most important skills you can have.

The most important advice I have ever received on writing is to:

Write like you talk.

One doesn't use fancy language when one is communicating verbally, so why do the same when writing? If you have trouble writing naturally, try recording yourself and transcribe the results afterwards.

"If it sounds like writing, I rewrite it."

– Elmore Leonard

Start with writing for yourself. When we write for ourselves, it helps us to think, learn, and understand. Writing for ourselves is a private affair, though later, it may be shared with others. And when you do, you open your writing to the public. Then you can write for assessment or publication for a wider readership.

I have gone out of my way to be fluently articulate. I read, I look up words, I learn synonyms. I have learned the syllables. I practise pronunciation. I am constantly challenging myself to learn more. Nothing like being in the driver's seat. Sometimes I say stuff and no one understands me. And when that happens, it gives me a moment to reflect.

I take a moment of pause to consider the difficulty in understanding from their point of view. They are the listener, and the message I am trying to communicate isn't getting through. At this moment, it's probably more important that

I focus on delivering my message in a way they can grasp, as I am writing for them. Or maybe I change my audience to those who are already there at my level.

Writing has taken multifaceted forms now. You no longer need a direct audience. It's spread everywhere. Writing has also become democratic. Social media posts, captions, and statuses have all entered the domain of writing. It moves, impacts, and also sells.

Democratic Writing

But are writers a chosen few? Or can anyone write?

The answer is anyone can write. Simply because everyone can feel, think, and express. They just need to be trained to convert those thoughts into words on paper. Do we need to enrol ourselves in a school to do that? No, the key is practice. And patience. And both. All you need is a sheet of paper and a pen. The only way to learn writing is by writing. Okay, but why can't I just speak? Won't that do the same? Help me convey my thoughts and express my feelings. No, there is a difference between speaking and writing.

Input = Output

Javed Akhtar was once asked, 'what's the practice of writing'? He famously answered, 'reading'. You can only write if you have read a lot. You need to have a rich vocabulary, an understanding of every word; its meaning, essence, cultural context, and how to use it in different situations. You should know how a 40-year-old would speak and how a Gen Z would speak. You have a lot of feelings, and when you know a lot of words for different feelings and emotions, you can express yourself diversely with the support of those words. For example, feeling anxious is different from feeling depressed, and feeling irritated is different from feeling frustrated. When you read a lot and also command a superior talent for writing, you develop a superpower of writing about anything and changing the thinking of millions. Once you have clarity in your thoughts, nobody can manipulate you into their thinking.

Writers perceive surroundings, people, news, and developments differently and can read between the lines. They can analyse the structure and look beyond that. Converting this into writing is the greatest use of the greatest power they have. People see how something is happening; writers see why something is happening. Pieces of writing have changed the course of history, unleashed feminism, brought war propaganda, launched social reform movements, and changed society for good. It has been used to talk about minorities, shed light on injustices, and create empathy and understanding between people. That is the pinnacle of writing. It's rare to reach that spot. And you don't have to set that as your standard. If you can, your name will be inscribed in golden letters. But if not, you will still go back with your head clear.

Writing is a muscle that keeps on expanding the more you write.

Heard once that writing comes out of desperation. You have feelings bursting out of your brain. It is physically hurting you. Your brain would erupt if you don't blurt it out. But sadly, you have no one around. So you look for a paper and write it down.

For letting someone know how they've hurt your feelings or abused your kindness.

Be you.

Writing is equal parts therapeutic and revealing.

How Books Influence Us

The books I have read have led me here: a place of better understanding about human nature, tolerance towards different viewpoints, and social systems.

We have not yet invented time travel, but travelling makes us telepathic. Anne Frank, through her book, took everyone to the Holocaust time. Khaled Hosseini with *A Thousand Splendid Suns* made us cry over the state of Afghanistan.

Think of Plato, Da Vinci, Shakespeare, and Darwin. We know about history's great thinkers because they took the trouble to write things down.

When we read a sad book, our brains may activate the medial prefrontal cortex, allowing us to empathise with the characters and their emotions. This activation of the medial prefrontal cortex can also trigger the release of oxytocin, a hormone that is associated with social bonding and emotional attachment.

When we write, we get caught in the maze of literary praise. That becomes our sole driving force. But don't let it distract you. Write for the sake of writing. You serve the craft; the craft doesn't serve you. And the craft, in turn, serves others. C.S. Lewis said it well: "Child, to say the very thing you really mean, the whole of it, nothing more or less or other than what you really mean; that's the whole art and joy of words."

A writer's job is to witness. The more I write, the more I see the story in everything.

I love the challenge of writing. I love seeing something and thinking, "How do I capture this moment in words?" I ask myself, "Will anyone care about this story?" "Does it have a message, or am I just overthinking?" And then I am reminded that everything is a story. We are humans in story form.

And when I find the right words to describe that exactly, I feel like a wizard who pulls a rabbit out of his hat. I doubt if I am a wizard with magical powers and could go to Hogwarts. And J.K. Rowling has created such a fantastic world that it is easier to be convinced of its truth. When I highlight certain words, I feel like I am an influencer who can shed light on specific words and make them more important than others. I can shift people's focus on some things more than others, almost to the point of being unfair. Look at me, I can change people's religious views and political affiliations.

When I hit space and full stop on my keyboard, I feel like a warrior sharpening my weapons.

I love the emotional reactions I receive from my writing. I love getting messages that say "you changed the way I think" or "that was so powerful" or "that was exactly what I needed to hear". That's my job as a writer, and so I love it when it works.

It is not always a pretty process. Very frustrating at times, irritating in some ways. But I love this method of creation because I suck at all other forms of self-expression. I love making people laugh.

I like being critiqued, contested, and opposed because my writing becomes a ground for new debate and opinions to be created. I write because nobody has to read, but everyone can.

Writing is my sanctuary. I get to decide whom to allow to enter and whom not to. No expectations, no pressure. It's my private conversation; however, it somehow resonates with other people as their own. I started with walking alone, but soon I had a caravan of followers with me. I am soon talking to them through my books, at their homes, offices, airports, cafes, cars, and in bedrooms.

Commitment is Key

Writing transcends one-sided communication; it's an intimate dance between author and reader. Words become tender whispers, forging bonds between strangers.

"They can love it, they can hate it, but it should not confuse anybody." Great philosophy for anything creative/ artistic.

Just by committing yourself to writing two pages a day, you can develop inner clarity and conscience. Developing a habit of listening to your heart ensures long-term success in all fronts of life.

Read books that make you go 'huh' and challenge your knowledge. Lawyers, poets, and classic writers are your guiding light here.

If possible, write with your hand. Writing with your hand is like a therapy session minus the coach. Your hand becomes an extension of your body, and your body gets in on the action. You will write down the demons on the paper and see it shrink to the level of insects as soon as you finish writing. And if it's a bad memory, just throw out that paper, burn it, or flush it down. There are high chances that bad memories would be erased. Handwriting helps you focus and turn off that monkey mind. Don't worry about spellings or grammar. Writing psychology also agrees with it. Start small; you don't have to become the next Samuel Pepys or Anne Frank. It's your secret locked diary.

It helps you please your thoughts at a particular moment, and you can always revise it yourself and compare what kind of person you were at that time. It's like time travelling.

Using Raps, Quotes and Proverbs

I remember, while growing up, my mom had a knack of using the right proverbs at the right time. And I used to tease her, saying she should write them all down in a notebook and give it to me. I noticed she could convey it in one sentence, which takes people paragraphs to do. A proverb is compressed knowledge that conveys the exact meaning in a few words. It is funny, eccentric, and also taunting. It is the ultimate play of words. One sentence contains within it the entire culture and history of that sentence. And the beauty is that you need to know the cultural context to understand the meaning. You need to be exposed to it culturally and geographically to understand it. Let's take a proverb as an example: "Bandar kya jaane adrak ka swaad."

(Literal: "What does a monkey know of the wonderful taste of ginger?" This means that it needs a connoisseur to understand the worth of something. Its English equivalent is: 'casting pearls before swine'. Throwing pearls at pigs is of no use because they won't know that they are valuable. Monkeys never taste ginger, so they would never know how good they taste. Just like pigs won't know the value of pearls.)

Another one is 'Chiragh Taley Andhera'. It originates from a factual situation. Just look for a "Chiragh", a kerosene lamp or wax lamp. You will find darkness just underneath at the base of the lamp. Its English matching idiom could be "Nearer to the church, farther from heaven". Now church and heaven are two different concepts, which are difficult to be understood in Indian society. But Indians would all understand what a 'chiragh' or a kerosene lamp looks like.

At the end of the day, if you want people to hear about your business, you should write. If you care about sharing and improving ideas, you should write and above all…If you want to find your voice and understand yourself, you should write. Writing creates an amazing feedback loop that enhances everything you do. Of all the life changes I've written about over the past few years, the most transformative has been the writing itself. And it was only when I came to write this book (which was originally a talk) that I realised this. Of course, I'm not the first person to recognise this…

I'd argue that the cognitive shift in going from an audience of zero (talking to yourself) to an audience of 10 (a few friends or random strangers checking out your online post) is so big that it's actually huger than going from 10 people to a million.

Clive Thompson (Writer for The New York Times and Wired magazine).

Writing doesn't just help you; it can also help anyone who reads what you've written. And I promise you that you'll have more to say than you think, even if it's tricky to extract your thoughts.

Think of an artist who's just started painting. He wouldn't worry about organising an exhibition until he had some great work to show. It's the same with writing. Don't worry about how you're going to find readers, which blogging platform to use, or which text editor to use. Your chief concern should be listening to yourself (not just "yourself", but your inner self) and then writing as often as possible; carving out time in your week to sit down without distractions and write something.

(Just some of the) reasons you should write:

Nobody has ever seen literature in the same way as before, after William Shakespeare showed us a revolutionary path.

Leonardo da Vinci changed the whole perspective of the painting genre with his hugely influential work in that arena.

The greatest impact you can have as an artist is to make a mark, introduce a new era in your field. If you can change the point of view of people and make them see things the way you see it, there is nothing more satisfying than that. Art is powerful - at least potentially - almost beyond our imagination. Why? Because it is capable of reaching the stored reserves of a human being, the mysterious capacities of humanity which we do not even consciously know or fully understand. These capacities and their connection to art, particularly in the form of music and storytelling, have helped human beings to survive terrible circumstances and tragedies.

Biggest advantage of the Internet is its algorithm - it's like a virtual library stacked with similar books. Once you google something and the internet knows you are interested in it, it will show you everything related to it with one click and then just refresh it and use it to your advantage. - It will become Watson to your Sherlock Holmes and do the hard work of digging up information and content for it.

Write down what you think - do it every day for 15 minutes - in 10 years, your thinking would be straightened out.

You should always know more than what you are saying. And when you are not able to write, that means you haven't read about it a lot. That is a signal for you to start writing more on that topic, and especially to fill the gaps you are encountering.

Helps you in negotiation - this is what success is - being able to negotiate.

We have now established that writing is pretty cool and effective as well. So, why aren't we doing it more?

Because we think it belongs to an exclusive club of gifted writers. And the membership is by talent, which we do not possess. Or, I don't want to make a career in publishing books, so there is no need for me to write. These are all myths. Writing is a habit. It has nothing to do with your professional life. We can't publish a book. But we don't have to. Oh, let's learn how to find space for writing in our daily routine. We are not that busy to write because it is just one of the modes of communication. We use other modes of communication throughout the day, like speaking and listening; it's just that we have to understand and practise how to inculcate the third and the most important form of communication, that is writing also in our daily routine.

Do I need to learn 'writing' in today's age of AI?

There is no denying that AI has been a big leap in technological advancement. What used to take hours and manpower of hundreds of people is now being done at one click by AI. It has also taken over creative works like editing, story writing, content creation, photography, video creation, making presentations, etc. There is a danger that it might take over human imagination and creativity. And since you can get anything written by it by just giving a clear prompt, it has led to further undervaluation of writing in people's minds. Yes, it has made it easier but it can definitely not replace human imagination. Firstly, you need to know how to write in a clear, concise and brief manner to give a relevant prompt for the desired results. So you still need writing. And secondly and most importantly, it can never replace genuine human writing, at least not today. AI's writing is robotic and monotonous. There are certain phrases which are repeated everywhere because AI feeds on vast amounts of text as its fodder. It then picks out the most common phrases and uses them everywhere. So, unless you are very careful with your prompts, it would deliver a robotic, repetitive result.

Also, the jargon it uses is very technical, polished, and difficult. It might sound fancy, but our human brains can't make much sense of it. Our brains can only remember content that has made sense to us, moved our hearts, or was simple to understand. There has to be a human touch to it. Writing has to be simple. It has to have a unique voice. And AI cannot bring this uniqueness. And if you want to do some personal writing, AI would not be able to put into words what you are thinking and feeling. Even if you tell AI that you are feeling anxious, it would never be able to describe 'your anxiety'. AI is definitely a great tool to help you out when you get stuck at something, rephrase sentences for you, find better words and search things, but it still cannot replace the raw, honest, imperfect, deeply moving, and unique human writing.

PART 4

LET'S START WRITING

It is always said that the only way to write better is to write more. So, let's see how we can squeeze some writing into our daily life.

1. **Journaling**

    It probably is the oldest and often-cited method of writing. You take a diary and vent out your feelings on it, literally, blurt it out. No one has access to it, and it becomes your safe haven. Journaling has also been clinically proven to deal with anxiety, depression, and other mental health disorders. When I journal, I do it to hear myself, to let me know that I am valued and accepted by myself, if not for anyone else. It's the closest I have been to feeling alive.

2. **Make a To-do List with the Idea of Completing It**

    Reflect on the thought behind it rather than recording the events.

    Aren't we all meant to make a to-do list the first thing in the morning to keep a tab on how to run errands or emails to be returned, things to buy, bills to pay, diet to follow? We all make to-do lists, so let's give a small twist to it. Instead of just methodologically writing one-word actions to be completed in a day, we can start by writing the intent behind that action and the purpose behind completing it, or simply why it is important and how it would make you feel. It could just be one line or a couple of lines, but it would set the ball rolling and get you into the habit of assessing your thoughts, actions, and emotions behind it. The more you're able to express these emotions on a piece of paper, the better you would get at reflecting your inner emotions and projecting them outwards.

For the ultimate immersive experience, dive deep into your thoughts.

3. **For Expressing Love**

For expressing love, 'Words of affirmation' is one of the five love languages we have, and surprisingly, it is mine as well. Oh, it is a different joy to receive love letters, birthday cards, and postcards from your friends when they have travelled abroad, anniversary notes, apology letters, or just a simple thank you note. It is a human touch, a personal touch, which automatically makes you like the other person a little more, makes them appear sincere, and produces happy hormones in you when you read it. If you are a hoarder like me, you would also preserve all the birthday cards and notes that have ever been given to you by anybody. That's the strange thing about cards. It drives you back to that exact moment and feeling which you felt when you first received it, and the best feeling is when you randomly stumble upon that card while finding something else in the cupboard, and it takes you back to that nostalgic time.

So if this is what you feel when you receive it, this is how the other person also feels when they receive it, so please get into the habit of writing more personalised notes to people every day. Be it for something as simple as a thank you, for a sweet gesture such as thank you for cooking your favourite meal, a sorry for being late or being rude, a proud of you card for the smallest achievements which you can keep in their lunch bag, office bag, paste it on the fridge, keep it on the dining table or the work desk, bedside table, paste it on their laptop sleeve, or give them a full handwritten note with a bunch of flowers. And see the magic unravel in your life. You will see drastic improvements in your relationship.

I know we are living in a social media age. This means this list can be extended to digital writing, such as WhatsApping someone's wishes and congratulations, writing status updates about them, tweets, emails, etc.

4. **Gratitude List: Should I Feel It, Say It, or Write It?**

Expressing gratitude is the easiest way to feel contentment in life; however, we do it the wrong way. We know that we have to feel grateful, so we say it out loud that I am happy, I'm peaceful, I'm lucky to have these people in my life, I'm happy with my job, etc. But we don't feel it. We don't feel it to the extent that the energy or the vibration of the thoughts, which are in the inner part of our mind, for it to actually rewire our thinking system, and that is where writing plays a pivotal part. When you feel gratitude and you write the same thing in a notebook 10x20 times, it goes directly into your brain enough for your brain and body to feel that energy.

This brings me to my next point which is to keep a gratitude journal where every day you write things you're grateful for and the next day before starting a new page; you read the last one and the cycle continues. It's difficult for you to remember the thought you had yesterday when you were expressing gratitude to them, but it's easy to remember that thought when you read it again in the notebook and feel the gratitude again. It also helps you remember that this is not a problem because yesterday you were grateful for this very thing. At night when you're reading your gratitude journal, you see that two days ago you had written that you're grateful for the flexibility this job provides you and the stability of income that it gives you in order to take care of your family and organise your bills. So when you read that, it certainly helps you remember that all yesterday you were grateful for this thing which you are not able to see today because you are angry at other things in the office, and it immediately shifts your mind to the positive side of your job. Cataloguing your gratitude list is a great idea. It helps in not getting carried away by negative thoughts, and once you have revised it a couple of times, it all becomes part of your subconscious thinking, where the change happens, and your new thinking builds on this positivity, and a grateful framework develops in your body.

5.   Catching Ideas

Humans have 70,000 thoughts per day. We are always thinking about something. Whenever we are driving somewhere, listening to songs, walking to somebody, what we have is almost a lightbulb moment where we have a beautiful thought, like a vision about something, observation about something or something just suddenly makes sense which we were trying to figure out for so many days. But you just forget that thought and never think of it again. But it's better to quickly write down the thought in your notepad or keep a diary handy if you have it, and I know at times you will see that you would have a diary or a notepad full of beautiful ideas which will help you reflect back; would make you feel that you are so intelligent to have such profound ideas and sometimes when you are looking at something else the previous idea would help you connect the dots and make sense of the bigger picture. It also helps you present those thoughts in parties, dinner table conversations, team meetings, family gatherings or just while talking to your friends you can also use it. You can also use it for your social media captions or use it in your YouTube videos if you are interested in making one. It is, in general, going to enrich your conversations with people and improve the quality of your thoughts.

6. **Reflective Notes**

Reflective notes are made when you listen/watch something and then reflect upon it.

It could be in various ways like movie reviews, social media posts about political analysis, football match, cricket match reviews, restaurant reviews, food reviews, place reviews, car reviews, technological gadgets reviews, movie recommendations, location recommendations, etc. Trust me, the best publicity is the word of mouth publicity. When you write about something and convey it to others, it is bound to persuade others more.

7.   Words of Affirmation

My first exposure to understanding manifestation was when I read the book *The Secret.* That book moved me to tears and completely changed my thinking. It was one of those pivotal moments where I had paradigmatic shifts in life. It was a watershed moment where my thinking completely changed. I was earlier part of the destiny club, and then I started believing that I could also control my own destiny. Then I studied a lot about manifestation. I realised there are different ways of practising it. One of the ways is by words of affirmation, so it's when you write down something that you want to manifest in clear words a hundred times until you start feeling the vibrancy of the words when you read it. You could also imagine everything you want in the future and manifest it through words.

Conclusion

This book is all about my passion for writing and love for the world it creates.

I firmly believe, today, more than ever is the age of words. Today is the age of ideas, and we are in the middle of a knowledge revolution. Ideas are the seeds of knowledge. An idea so great that it stops you in your tracks. How do you find that idea? There are hundred ways of doing it, and one of them is writing. Surprisingly, it's the most mundane and common way of doing it. It's a practice that will yield results when you need it the most.

Society was built on the back of the stories we tell. So tell yours.

We don't live in a world of scarcity. We live in a world of abundance. I want everyone to feel creative satisfaction. There's no excuse not to. Take advantage of all the opportunities, and then pay it forward by helping others.

The End

"Writing sets me free."

– Alice Walker

www.ingramcontent.com/pod-product-compliance
Lightning Source LLC
Chambersburg PA
CBHW021136130726
47988CB00003B/1336